TRANSFOR...
OF A ...

SEX

John D. Pierce
and Stephen W. Smith

SIX SESSIONS FOR INDIVIDUALS OR GROUPS

IVP Connect

An imprint of InterVarsity Press
Downers Grove, Illinois

InterVarsity Press
P.O. Box 1400, Downers Grove, IL 60515-1426
World Wide Web: www.ivpress.com
E-mail: mail@ivpress.com

InterVarsity Press® is the book-publishing division of InterVarsity Christian Fellowship/USA®, a student movement active on campus at hundreds of universities, colleges and schools of nursing in the United States of America, and a member movement of the International Fellowship of Evangelical Students. For information about local and regional activities, write Public Relations Dept., InterVarsity Christian Fellowship/USA, 6400 Schroeder Rd., P.O. Box 7895, Madison, WI 53707-7895, or visit the IVCF website at <www.intervarsity.org>.

Portions of this guide are adapted from The Transformation of a Man's Heart, ©2006 by Stephen W. Smith.

Design: Cindy Kiple
Images: Gen Nishino / Getty Images

ISBN-10: 0-8308-2146-5
ISBN-13: 978-0-8308-2146-4

Printed in the United States of America ∞

P	19	18	17	16	15	14	13	12	11	10	9	8	7	6	5	4	3	2	1
Y	21	20	19	18	17	16	15	14	13	12	11	10	09	08	07	06				

CONTENTS

INTRODUCTION

Too often we are like strangers in our own house. Asked why we think, feel and act in a certain way, we find we have no answer.

Consider, for example, our sexuality. We're told that we think about sex every eleven seconds, but for all that thinking we can't really articulate why we long for love, for connection. We can't recount the story of our sexuality in such a way that we see the greater story being told in our lives. We allow our sexuality to inform our minds and our bodies, but we can keep it safely cordoned off from our hearts.

The journey toward transformation is all about reshaping our hearts; not the muscle in our chest but what Henri Nouwen calls "our hidden center"—often hidden even from us. We keep our distance from it, as though what holds the passion inside of us is what frightens us most.

That is the painful part of being human. We fail to know our hidden center and our submerged parts, so we live and die without knowing who we really are. We are strangers in our own house.

The four Transformation of a Man's Heart discussion guides help us to get our house in order. More than just a Bible study, these guides help us to explore the distinctives of the masculine heart and move us toward authentic transformation into the men God wants us to become.

Each session begins with an excerpt from the book *The Transformation of a Man's Heart,* compiled and edited by Stephen W. Smith.

This passage can be read individually or aloud in a group setting. It isn't necessary to read the book before going through this guide, but you may want to read the book for a more in-depth exploration of how God transforms a man's life.

Sessions are divided into five different sections, each of which helps you focus on a different aspect of your heart. "Examining My Story" offers reflective questions and exercises that help prepare us for the topic, theme and heartfelt need that will be addressed. "Engaging the Scriptures" is a guided study of a particular section of Scripture with questions and comments. "Experiencing the Journey" is a practical application of what has just been studied.

This convergence of thought, Scripture and reflection will help equip us for what lies ahead. "Expressing Our Hearts to God" offers creative ways of praying about the subject. And occasional "Encouragements from Other Companions" run alongside each session to reassure us that our experience is authentic and transformation is possible.

SUGGESTIONS FOR INDIVIDUAL USE

If you have chosen to use this guide individually, you can move at your own pace from session to session, taking as much time as you like working through the questions, journaling your responses and taking notes. Consider using a simple spiral-bound journal to elaborate on your answers. Allow yourself to reflect on the issues that are raised. Each session is designed to be a guided journey into the truth of God's Word and the issues of a man's heart.

1. As you begin each session, pray that God will speak to you through his Word.

2. Read the introduction to the session and respond to the personal reflection questions under "Examining My Story." These are designed to help you focus on God and on the theme of the session.

3. "Engaging the Scriptures" deals with a particular biblical passage. Read and reread the passage to be studied. Unless otherwise indicated, the questions are written using the language of the New International Version, so you may wish to use that version of the Bible. *The Message* is also recommended.

4. It might be good to have a Bible dictionary handy. Use it to look up any unfamiliar words, names or places.

5. Take your time working through "Experiencing the Journey." The witness of the Bible and the work of the Spirit may converge in your heart during this time. Be honest with yourself and open to change.

6. Use the prayer suggestion to guide you in thanking God for what you have learned and to pray about the applications that have come to mind.

SUGGESTIONS FOR GROUP MEMBERS

Small groups and classes make excellent forums for rich discussion; this guide will help a group get to some of the core issues facing men today. Lively discussion should be welcomed, and every member of your group should strive to create a safe environment for each other to share openly and deeply about issues of the heart.

A safe environment for men is fostered by setting certain ground rules which should be agreed on prior to the group's beginning. Here are some suggested ground rules to think through prior to beginning your group:

1. Be willing to participate in the discussion. The leader will be asking the questions that are found in this guide. The leader can really become more of a guide than a teacher, helping navigate the discussion that will result from the study. The sessions will "teach" themselves. Group members will also help teach each other.

2. Stick to the topic being discussed. This allows for everyone to par-

ticipate in in-depth study on equal ground.

3. Be sensitive to the other members of the group. Listen attentively when they describe what they have learned. You may be surprised by their insights! Many questions do not have "right" answers, particularly questions that aim at meaning or application.

4. Jesus modeled acceptance throughout his interaction with people. Paul reminds us to "accept one another just as Christ accepted you" (Romans 15:7). Feeling accepted without the threat of feeling judged is key to helping men relax and share their story and heart struggles. In the group, be affirming whenever you can. This will encourage some of the more hesitant members of the group to participate.

5. Be careful not to dominate the discussion. We are sometimes so eager to express our thoughts that we leave too little opportunity for others to respond. By all means participate! But allow others to also. Everyone needs to be heard, and if we can make sure that all hearts are heard when we do the study, we'll meet a deeper goal of actually being a "group" or community.

6. Expect God to teach you through the passage being discussed and through the other members of the group. Pray that you will have an enjoyable and profitable time together, but also that as a result of each session you will find ways that you can participate in God's work transforming your life.

7. Confidentiality is important to create a safe environment. Decide together who the group members will tell. Will spouses or other friends know what is shared in the group? Anything said in the group should not be discussed outside the group unless specific permission is given to do so.

If you are the group leader, you will find additional suggestions and help at the back of the guide.

THE PROCESS OF TRANSFORMATION

Transformation is *never* complete. I am no trophy of transformation, only a man in the process of transformation. I can only confess (and you can confess with me):

God uses flawed men to accomplish his purposes.
I am a flawed man.
I am a man in process.
God is using me now and will continue to use me in the future to accomplish what he desires.
I am not perfect, but I am available.
Come, O God, and transform my heart.

The real transformation of a man involves his heart. If we are to be transformed, God must have access to that sacred place within. Let the transformation begin!

ONE

THE CREATION OF SEX

Our deepest longings to be admired, wanted, respected and loved are revealed in our sex lives. Also exposed are our greatest battles with foolishness, ill motive and sin. Our sexual pursuits or evasions uncover the mix and mire that is intertwined in our heart, revealing the temptation to be selfish and demanding or the honorable desires to be sacrificial and loving. The Scriptures give us great clarity about many sexual dos and don'ts, but there are few simple answers for the myriad of sexual questions many of us would face if our own sexual dramas were put under the microscope.

EXAMINING MY STORY

1. Finish these sentences for yourself and share what you feel comfortable with in the group:

   For me sex means . . .

   Sex makes me feel . . .

   This study is making me feel . . .

2. What relationships, events or cultural influences helped shape your understanding of your sex?

ENGAGING THE SCRIPTURES

Genesis 1:26-28; 2:18-25

[26] Then God said, "Let us make man in our image, in our likeness, and let them rule over the fish of the sea and the birds of the air, over the livestock, over all the earth, and over all the creatures that move along the ground."

> [27] So God created man in his own image,
>   in the image of God he created him;
>   male and female he created them.

[28] God blessed them and said to them, "Be fruitful and increase in number; fill the earth and subdue it. Rule over the fish of the sea and the birds of the air and over every living creature that moves on the ground."

[18] The LORD God said, "It is not good for the man to be alone. I will make a helper suitable for him."

[19] Now the LORD God had formed out of the ground all the beasts of the field and all the birds of the air. He brought them to the man to see what he would name them; and whatever the man called each living creature, that was its name. [20] So the man

gave names to all the livestock, the birds of the air and all the beasts of the field.

But for Adam no suitable helper was found. [21]So the LORD God caused the man to fall into a deep sleep; and while he was sleeping, he took one of the man's ribs and closed up the place with flesh. [22]Then the LORD God made a woman from the rib he had taken out of the man, and he brought her to the man.

[23]The man said,

> "This is now bone of my bones
> and flesh of my flesh;
> she shall be called 'woman,'
> for she was taken out of man."

[24]For this reason a man will leave his father and mother and be united to his wife, and they will become one flesh.

[25]The man and his wife were both naked, and they felt no shame.

3. From the passages, list as many purposes for sex as you can.

4. Why do you think God declared it "not good" for the man to be alone?

Sex is the closest that many people ever come to a spiritual experience. Indeed, it is because it is a spiritual experience of sorts that so many chase after it with a repetitive, desperate kind of abandon. Often, whether they know it or not, they are searching for God.

SCOTT PECK

---

5. Why would no suitable helper be found among the animals? What makes human beings unique?

6. Which is the greater cure for loneliness—companionship or sex? Explain.

7. In Genesis 2:24, notice the progression of a man leaving, uniting and becoming one flesh. What reason does the previous passage supply for this progression?

8. How is sexual intimacy affected when this progression is not followed?

You will never have a marriage (or relationship) pleasing to God until you comprehend who you are and who you were meant to become. To understand yourself, one must begin to comprehend the wonder of what it means to be made in the image of God.

DAN ALLENDER

Experiencing the Journey

9. After considering the passages above, what do you assume God's mood is toward sex?

10. What does being "naked" and feeling "no shame" look like for you?

11. Where are you on the journey toward God's ideal?

EXPRESSING OUR HEARTS TO GOD

The Naked Man's Prayer

God, thank you that I am gloriously and creatively made, with strength and passion to honor your great name. There is nothing that can protect me but your watchful eyes. Naked I stand before you acknowledging that you have given me the senses to know your pleasure and glory.

You have given me the eyes to behold what is enticing, stunning, arousing and pleasurable. Thank you that I want to see and be seen.

You have given me the ears to hear what I long to hear: "Well done," "I love you," "I want you," "I need you," "You matter to me" . . . Thank you that I want to hear and be heard.

You have given me the scent of the open air of heaven and all the aromas that are stirred by your love. Thank you that the scent of love brings joy to my heart.

You have given me a hunger to taste and see that you are truly good.

You have given me the desire to touch and be touched—and this desire is from you.

Lord, I confess that my senses have led to places far from you.

Please clothe me with the garments of Christ, so that I can walk with no shame.

THE FALL OF SEX

It does not take much when you look around to realize that our understanding of sex has become terribly distorted. The way we look at it, what we expect from it, why we are even writing about it is proof that something has gone wrong. Before the Fall, sex was most likely deeply enjoyed like every good gift the Father had given, but hardly something that would get the attention it does today. Since the Fall, when Adam and Eve were banished from the garden and their eyes were opened to their exposure, the Bible traces the marred sexual stories of God's people.

The problem is not new. Something happened to us in the garden that changed everything and in this instance, changed our view and experience of sex.

EXAMINING MY STORY

1. Think of the experiences (relationships, conversations, events, etc.) that have shaped your sexual story. With one or two of the remembered instances, draw something to represent it. Do your best not to use any words, just drawings.

ENGAGING THE SCRIPTURES

Genesis 19:1-13

[1]The two angels arrived at Sodom in the evening, and Lot was sitting in the gateway of the city. When he saw them, he got up to meet them and bowed down with his face to the ground. [2]"My lords," he said, "please turn aside to your servant's house. You can wash your feet and spend the night and then go on your way early in the morning."

"No," they answered, "we will spend the night in the square."

[3]But he insisted so strongly that they did go with him and entered his house. He prepared a meal for them, baking bread without yeast, and they ate. [4]Before they had gone to bed, all the men from every part of the city of Sodom—both young and old—surrounded the house. [5]They called to Lot, "Where are the men who came to you tonight? Bring them out to us so that we can have sex with them."

[6]Lot went outside to meet them and shut the door behind him [7]and said, "No, my friends. Don't do this wicked thing. [8]Look, I have two daughters who have never slept with a man. Let me bring them out to you, and you can do what you like with them. But don't do anything to these men, for they have come under the protection of my roof."

[9]"Get out of our way," they replied. And they said, "This fellow came here as an alien, and now he wants to play the judge! We'll treat you worse than them." They kept bringing pressure on Lot and

My husband is in love with his own body. . . . I have seen him nude, gesturing before a mirror. He gets the same pleasure out of that as in making love to me. I am not loved. I am merely a vessel through whom he loves himself.

A YOUNG WOMAN, QUOTED BY LEANNE PAYNE

moved forward to break down the door.

[10]But the men inside reached out and pulled Lot back into the house and shut the door. [11]Then they struck the men who were at the door of the house, young and old, with blindness so that they could not find the door.

[12]The two men said to Lot, "Do you have anyone else here—sons-in-law, sons or daughters, or anyone else in the city who belongs to you? Get them out of here, [13]because we are going to destroy this place. The outcry to the LORD against its people is so great that he has sent us to destroy it."

2. Imagine that you were in this scene. What would it have been like to be Lot? to be his daughters? to be one of the mob?

3. How do you think a guy like Lot got to be in a town like Sodom?

4. Read verses 6-9. Lot puts himself and his daughters at risk to protect the angels. Why do you think he would do this?

The harem [of our imagination] is always accessible, always subservient, calls for no sacrifices or adjustments, and can be endowed with erotic and psychological attractions that no real woman can rival. Among those shadowy brides he is always adored, always the perfect love, no demand is made on his unselfishness, no mortification ever imposed on his vanity. In the end, they become merely the medium through which he increasingly adores himself.

C. S. LEWIS

---

5. In what ways do you relate to Lot? to his daughters? to the mob?

Lust is the ape that gibbers in our loins. Tame him as we will by day, he rages all the wilder in our dreams by night. Just when we think we're safe from him, he raises up his ugly head and smirks, and there is no river in the world flows cold and strong enough to strike him down. Almighty God, why dost thou deck men out with such a loathsome toy?

FREDERICK
BUECHNER

6. In verses 10-11 the angels intervene. What safeguards does God provide us to protect us from sexual sin?

EXPERIENCING THE JOURNEY

7. What desires do you have that could be precursors to sexual sin?

8. Reflect on your recurrent sexual fantasies. What common themes (hunger for affirmation or admiration, control, anger, being pursued, etc.) can you identify? What do these themes reveal about the desires in your heart?

9. In what ways are these desires honorable? In what ways are they dangerous?

10. What people, places and activities in your life serve to safeguard your sexual integrity?

EXPRESSING OUR HEARTS TO GOD

The Naked Man's Prayer

Dear God, when you created me to be a sexual man, you did a powerful thing that I am trying to understand. How is it that you care about such deep things and want the best for me?

I am realizing some of the ways that I have settled for less.

I feel . . .

I am asking you to . . .

Your word says you can give us a clean heart and a right spirit. I'm asking you to give me a clean mind. But to be honest, there is fear within me to bring what is held in darkness to the light.

I know I need your help and I need the encouragement of my friends to stand with me. I am asking for help outside of myself because I know that I cannot do this alone. I stand naked in my heart before you; weak in my efforts to change old ways; needy in my attempt to change again and yet desperate enough to ask you again for help.

THE REDEMPTION OF SEX

God desires to bring us through Christ the opportunity to become more fully ourselves: better warriors, lovers, friends and unique reflections of his likeness. Taking a closer look at your own sexual story can reveal the questions of your heart. It is a journey worth traveling.

EXAMINING MY STORY

1. Describe how you think belief in God makes a difference in a person's sexual life.

2. How might a person's sexuality reflect the character of God?

3. Who do you talk to about sex? What makes you uncomfortable in such conversations?

ENGAGING THE SCRIPTURES

1 Corinthians 6:9-20

[9]Do you not know that the wicked will not inherit the kingdom of God? Do not be deceived: Neither the sexually immoral nor idolaters nor adulterers nor male prostitutes nor homosexual offenders [10]nor thieves nor the greedy nor drunkards nor slanderers nor swindlers will inherit the kingdom of God. [11]And that is what some of you were. But you were washed, you were sanctified, you were justified in the name of the Lord Jesus Christ and by the Spirit of our God.

[12]"Everything is permissible for me"—but not everything is beneficial. "Everything is permissible for me"—but I will not be mastered by anything. [13]"Food for the stomach and the stomach for food"—but God will destroy them both. The body is not meant for sexual immorality, but for the Lord, and the Lord for the body. [14]By his power God raised the Lord from the dead, and he will raise us also. [15]Do you not know that your bodies are members of Christ himself? Shall I then take the members of Christ and unite them with a prostitute? Never! [16]Do you not know that he who unites himself with a prostitute is one with her in body? For it is said, "The two will become one flesh." [17]But he who unites himself with the Lord is one with him in spirit.

[18]Flee from sexual immorality. All other sins a man commits are outside his body, but he who sins sexually sins against his own body. [19]Do you not

know that your body is a temple of the Holy Spirit, who is in you, whom you have received from God? You are not your own; [20]you were bought at a price. Therefore honor God with your body.

4. Verses 9-10 identify a mix of sexual and nonsexual sins. What links these behaviors?

5. How might a person be deceived about the acceptability of these behaviors?

6. Read verse 11. What has changed for Paul's audience? How might Paul's statement make it easier for us to share our sexual stories?

7. Read verses 12-13. What conclusions might people draw about sinful behavior based on Paul's statement in verse 11?

8. What are contemporary examples of people say-

Only if a man finds that he is already accepted in his sin and sickness, can he accept his own self-preoccupation as it is; and only then can his psychic economy be opened toward others, to accept them as they are.

BRENNAN MANNING

ing "Everything is permissible for me?" How might Paul respond to people today?

> The number-one purpose of sex is neither procreation nor recreation, but unification. . . . This unification is the celebration of the soul-deep bond that is present when a couple knows and experiences the certainty that they are together, permanently, for a divine purpose.
>
> TIM ALAN GARDENER

9. Read verse 18. How does a relationship with Christ affect how we treat our bodies?

EXPERIENCING THE JOURNEY

10. How could God help you honor him with your body?

11. How could other men support you in discerning when something permissible is beginning to master you? What would this require of you? Of the group?

EXPRESSING OUR HEARTS TO GOD

The Naked Man's Prayer

O God, you know all things. My nakedness exposes me to the light and you see. There's no part of me, including my body, that I can hide from you. My sin is before me and before you. I'm sick of the shame I feel. I'm weighted down by the guilt.

It's like I live in a tomb; how can I get out? I'm tangled up in grave clothes of shame, blame and guilt. I want to walk forward. I want to walk toward you.

Knowing that you love my body makes me stop and think. Am I so "fearfully and wonderfully made" that you would even consider my body's redemption? Realizing that you care about what I do with my body humbles me, makes me pause and think, causes me to question what I do.

Calling you "Savior" means more than I have thought. My body is included in that confession. Lord, I need your salvation in every part: my eyes, my ears, my desires, my passion—every beat of my heart, if the truth is known.

Redeem me. Let me be free of the filthy garments of shame; the drabby cloak of blame and the heavy collar of guilt. Only you have the power to dress me so that I stand before you as a righteous man.

TELLING YOUR SEXUAL STORY

When I first breached the silence that shrouded my sexual story, I had no sense as to how my maturity had been impeded by my wounds and sin. Nor did I have any conception that there was anything beyond the black and white parameters of sexual behaving. I vaguely knew as a young man that I did not measure up to God's standards because I was more often than not disobedient. And in my naive understanding of his view toward me, I believed God wanted flawlessness from me rather than what a good Father would want for his son: maturing progress.

EXAMINING MY STORY

1. Fold a piece of paper in half. On one side, make a chronological list (in 5-10 year increments) of everything that has had an impact on your sexuality over the years—for good or for bad. On the other side, make notes about your sexual history that only you will understand.

2. What are two things you would say you learned about your sexuality as a man from remembering your history?

ENGAGING THE SCRIPTURES

Psalm 51:1-13

[1]Have mercy on me, O God,
    according to your unfailing love;
according to your great compassion
    blot out my transgressions.
[2]Wash away all my iniquity
    and cleanse me from my sin.
[3]For I know my transgressions,
    and my sin is always before me.
[4]Against you, you only, have I sinned
    and done what is evil in your sight,
so that you are proved right when you speak
    and justified when you judge.
[5]Surely I was sinful at birth,
    sinful from the time my mother conceived me.
[6]Surely you desire truth in the inner parts;
    you teach me wisdom in the inmost place.
[7]Cleanse me with hyssop, and I will be clean;
    wash me, and I will be whiter than snow.
[8]Let me hear joy and gladness;
    let the bones you have crushed rejoice.
[9]Hide your face from my sins
    and blot out all my iniquity.
[10]Create in me a pure heart, O God,
    and renew a steadfast spirit within me.
[11]Do not cast me from your presence
    or take your Holy Spirit from me.
[12]Restore to me the joy of your salvation
    and grant me a willing spirit, to sustain me.

13Then I will teach transgressors your ways,
   and sinners will turn back to you.

3. This passage is introduced as King David's confession of adultery, which involved a pregnancy. What do we know about David simply by reading this introduction?

4. Read verses 1-2. What is David hoping for from God?

5. Read verse 4. Why does David say he's sinned against God only by committing adultery? Who else is hurt by adultery?

6. Read verses 5-6. How might the understanding that we were sinful at birth help us make sense of our sexual story?

Wallowing in shame, remorse, self-hatred, and guilt over real or imagined failings in our past lives . . . shows that we have not accepted the acceptance of Jesus Christ and thus have rejected the total sufficiency of his redeeming work. . . . In order to grow in trust, we must allow God to see us and love us precisely as we are. The best way to do that is through prayer. As we pray, the unrestricted love of God gradually transforms us.

BRENNAN MANNING

7. How is David restored in this passage? How does a person stay connected to God after sexual sin?

8. Read verse 9. What does it say about God that David asks him to "hide your face from my sins"? What does it say about David?

To forgive another person [even ourselves] from the heart is an act of liberation.

HENRI NOUWEN

9. How does God help us get back to a state of being "pure," "steadfast," "willing" and filled with "joy"?

EXPERIENCING THE JOURNEY

10. How hard is it for you to talk to God about your sin?

11. What do you know about God that might make talking to him about your sin easier?

EXPRESSING OUR HEARTS TO GOD

The Naked Man's Prayer

Jesus, why is it that I am so often led to confession? I can't escape the fact that there remain parts of me that are not yet transformed. Even in my trying, I hold out on you and my friends, holding in secret what I still do. You know I am in process. So, Lord, I invite you to enter as my Sacred Companion and as my Divine Friend.

Jesus, you are a man. You know the reality of a man's world and a man's heart. Help me navigate my way to your Way. Help me be found by the truth that will set my heart so lightly free. I want that. I need that and I am glad that you want this for me. There is no life for me apart from the life of Jesus Christ.

I am asking for the way, the truth and the life to be given me every day of my life, beginning right now; right here.

COUNTERFEIT SEX

We just need to read our junk e-mail to hear about the possibilities of sexual pleasures awaiting just a click away. Fantasy meetings on Internet chat rooms or the regular dates with pornography and masturbation are an alluring diversion to lonely singleness, difficult marriages, anger and stress that we believe should not be part of our lives. Inundated daily from all sides with the messages that encourage us to go for all we can get, we easily can be led to make our sexual happiness the point of living. After all, the message goes, "you can have it now; why wait for marriage?" "Why wait on your wife?" Isn't all sex just sex?

Something that is counterfeit is an imitation of something superior; it is not genuine. So what does this word have to do with sex? Is there a difference between the counterfeit sex that tempts us and the sex blessed in the Bible?

EXAMINING MY STORY

1. How would you define counterfeit sex? What qualifies as counterfeit sex?

2. What is the attraction of counterfeit sex? Why is it so widely promoted and practiced?

3. In what ways are you exposed to the allure of counterfeit sex? What is the net effect of such exposure?

> *The Christian attitude does not mean that there is anything wrong about sexual pleasure, any more than about the pleasure of eating. It means that you must not isolate that pleasure and try to get it by itself, any more than you ought to try to get the pleasures of taste without swallowing and digesting, by chewing things and spitting them out again.*
>
> **C.S. LEWIS**

ENGAGING THE SCRIPTURES

Proverbs 7:6-27

[6]At the window of my house
    I looked out through the lattice.
[7] I saw among the simple,
    I noticed among the young men,
    a youth who lacked judgment.
[8]He was going down the street near her corner,
    walking along in the direction of her house
[9]at twilight, as the day was fading,
    as the dark of night set in.
[10]Then out came a woman to meet him,
    dressed like a prostitute and with crafty intent.

[11](She is loud and defiant,
    her feet never stay at home;
[12]now in the street, now in the squares,
    at every corner she lurks.)

[13]She took hold of him and kissed him
    and with a brazen face she said:
[14]"I have fellowship offerings at home;
    today I fulfilled my vows.
[15]So I came out to meet you;
    I looked for you and have found you!
[16]I have covered my bed
    with colored linens from Egypt.
[17]I have perfumed my bed
    with myrrh, aloes and cinnamon.
[18]Come, let's drink deep of love till morning;
    let's enjoy ourselves with love!
[19]My husband is not at home;
    he has gone on a long journey.
[20]He took his purse filled with money
    and will not be home till full moon."

[21]With persuasive words she led him astray;
    she seduced him with her smooth talk.
[22]All at once he followed her
    like an ox going to the slaughter,
    like a deer stepping into a noose
[23]till an arrow pierces his liver,
    like a bird darting into a snare,
    little knowing it will cost him his life.

[24]Now then, my sons, listen to me;
    pay attention to what I say.
[25]Do not let your heart turn to her ways
    or stray into her paths.
[26]Many are the victims she has brought down;

her slain are a mighty throng.
²⁷Her house is a highway to the grave,
    leading down to the chambers of death.

4. Read verses 6-9. What evidence is given to sug-
    gest that the young man "lacked judgment"?

> Lust, like physical
> sex, points in only
> one direction.
> You cannot go back
> to a lower level
> and stay satisfied.
> Always you want
> more . . . lust
> does not satisfy;
> it stirs up.
>
> ANONYMOUS

5. How is the woman described in verses 10-13?
    Should the young man have been surprised at
    her proposition? Why or why not?

6. List the things offered and promised by the
    woman to the man (vv. 14-20). What in this de-
    scription would appeal to a man?

7. Read verses 21-23. Why might such behavior
    cost the young man his life? What might such a
    situation lead to?

8. Verses 24-27 sum up the harsh reality that Solomon is warning us about. Why do you feel the word "victim" is used here? How can a young man avoid becoming a victim?

EXPERIENCING THE JOURNEY

9. In what ways is pornography like the woman in Proverbs 7? Why is pornography so powerful and attractive?

For Jesus, sex was too good, too high, too holy, to be thrown away by cheap thoughts.

RICHARD FOSTER

10. List some other sexual behaviors common to our culture that might be considered counterfeit. Which ones would you consider counterfeit? Why?

11. What are some common elements that make a sexual practice counterfeit?

EXPRESSING OUR HEARTS TO GOD

The Naked Man's Prayer

Lord, I stand before you admitting that my heart is so easily pulled by images, voices and encounters that I have every day. I feel so weak; so incredibly vulnerable, naked in this area. Like the young man in Proverbs, I can be seduced so easily. Help me to hear your voice of love calling me and not the voice that is beckoning me to walk a path away from you. I know that I need to guard my heart if I am to walk towards you and not away from you. But honestly, God, to guard my heart well, I need your help to do it. Protect my heart from my own desires which come from a dark place within me. Defend me from the Evil One who lures me and seeks to trap me. Give me courage to fight this fight well, today. Give me grace to walk unashamed through this day. Give me, O Lord, friends who can cheer me on toward you and away from sin. I commit my eyes to you. I commit my ears to you. I commit my body to you. May my body and my heart bring you glory through Jesus' name. Amen

POSITIVELY SEXUAL

Perhaps your efforts at being responsibly sexual have been exhausted, but God's have not. Biblical story after story recounts circumstances that seem hopeless until God enters the picture. Without question, the more honest about his struggle a man becomes with God, himself and other trusted allies, the higher the likelihood of him finding health and healing.

Good communities can encourage our faith in Christ when our own faith wanes; they can offer us hope to continue on when our other nature begs us to do otherwise. Good friends in faith comfort, challenge and rekindle our hearts. No matter where you are on the path of reckoning with your sexual maturity, you can always find a way to offer a taste of Christ to those around you.

EXAMINING MY STORY

1. How has hope helped you move toward authentic, positive sexuality?

2. Who do you feel comfortable talking with about your sexual story? How might such people encourage your faith and strengthen your hope?

3. What gets in the way of talking to your friends
    about your sexual struggles?

ENGAGING THE SCRIPTURES

Song of Songs 4:1-10

[1]How beautiful you are, my darling!
    Oh, how beautiful!
    Your eyes behind your veil are doves.
    Your hair is like a flock of goats
    descending from Mount Gilead.
[2]Your teeth are like a flock of sheep just shorn,
    coming up from the washing.
    Each has its twin;
    not one of them is alone.
[3]Your lips are like a scarlet ribbon;
    your mouth is lovely.
    Your temples behind your veil
    are like the halves of a pomegranate.
[4]Your neck is like the tower of David,
    built with elegance;
    on it hang a thousand shields,
    all of them shields of warriors.
[5]Your two breasts are like two fawns,
    like twin fawns of a gazelle
    that browse among the lilies.
[6]Until the day breaks
    and the shadows flee,

I will go to the mountain of myrrh
 and to the hill of incense.
[7]All beautiful you are, my darling;
 there is no flaw in you.
[8]Come with me from Lebanon, my bride,
 come with me from Lebanon.
 Descend from the crest of Amana,
 from the top of Senir, the summit of Hermon,
 from the lions' dens
 and the mountain haunts of the leopards.
[9]You have stolen my heart, my sister, my bride;
 you have stolen my heart
 with one glance of your eyes,
 with one jewel of your necklace.
[10]How delightful is your love, my sister, my bride!
 How much more pleasing is your love than wine,
 and the fragrance of your perfume than
  any spice!

4. How well does this man know his beloved? What about her captures his imagination?

5. List the specific parts of this passage that reflect positive sexuality.

The Christian life is rarely "natural." Far from it. It is not natural to love your neighbor, or to turn the other cheek, or to forgive someone who has wronged you. In the same way, resisting sexual temptation—or any kind of temptation—is not the "natural" thing to do. Christianity runs counter to humanity's baser natural intentions. By God's grace, and with the help of the Holy Spirit and the body of Christ, Christians are called to resist what is wrong and do what is right, regardless of how "unnatural" it may seem by societal standards.

ALBERT Y. HSU

6. How does love "steal" a man's heart (v. 9)?

7. Sexual intimacy is described here as beautiful, joyful and sensual. What does this passage say about God's design for sexual intimacy?

8. How can you claim or reclaim these values as you move toward being positively sexual?

Sexuality and spirituality are not enemies but friends.

DONALD GOERGEN

EXPERIENCING THE JOURNEY

9. What ought sex to look like and feel like? How is it different from counterfeit sex?

10. In what specific ways do you need encouragement to live positively sexual?

EXPRESSING OUR HEARTS TO GOD

The Naked Man's Prayer

O God, thank you for the Song of Songs where I can read with my own eyes and sense with my own heart what you want for me. Believing that sex is both good and holy, I want to experience what you want me to experience. I long to know "the delight of love" that is described in the Song of Songs. Forgive me for delighting in so much that is less . . . so much that is counterfeit that spoils what you have designed. Free my heart from lesser loves and lesser ways to aspire to your desire for me. Make my sex holy and help me to be holy in my experience of being positively sexual.

Jesus, you were a man who was both holy and sexual. Yet you navigated this in a way that seems too high for me to attain. Give to me the wisdom and understanding that you experienced. Please give me patience as I move toward holy sex.

Help my heart to be transformed.

LEADER'S NOTES

Leading a group discussion can be an enjoyable and rewarding experience. But it can also be *scary*—especially if you've never done it before.

You don't need to be an expert on the Bible or a trained teacher to lead a Bible discussion. These studies are designed to be led easily. As a matter of fact, the flow of questions is so natural that you may feel that the studies lead themselves. Nevertheless, there are some important facts to know about group dynamics and encouraging discussion. The suggestions listed below should enable you to effectively and enjoyably fulfill your role as leader.

COMPONENTS OF SMALL GROUPS

A healthy small group should do more than study the Bible. There are four components to consider as you structure your time together.

Nurture. Small groups help us to grow in our knowledge and love of God. Bible study is important for making this happen.

Community. Small groups are a great place to develop deep friendships with other Christians. Allow time for informal interaction before and after each study. Plan activities and games that will help you get to know each other. Spend time having fun together.

Worship and prayer. Your study will be enhanced by spending time praising God together in prayer or song. Pray for each other's needs—and keep track of how God is answering prayer in your group. Ask God to help you to apply what you are learning together.

Outreach. Reaching out to others can be a practical way of applying what you are learning, and it will keep your group from becoming self-focused. Consider together what other men in your lives would benefit from your group experience, and encourage participants to invite and welcome newcomers at appropriate moments in the life of your group.

PREPARING FOR THE STUDY

1. Pray for the various members of the group—including yourself. Ask God to open your hearts to the message of his Word and motivate you to action.

2. As you prepare for each session, read and reread the assigned Bible passage to familiarize yourself with it. Look at the passage in multiple translations; you can do so quickly by using Bible Gateway online <www.biblegateway.com>.

3. Carefully work through each question in the session. Spend some time alone sitting quietly before God, asking him to lead you into creative ways of guiding the group and even your own heart.

4. Write your thoughts and responses in the space provided in the guide. This will help you to express yourself clearly.

5. It might help to have a Bible dictionary handy. Use it to look up any unfamiliar words, names or places.

6. Remember that the group will follow your lead in responding to these sessions. They will not go any deeper than you do.

7. Once you have finished your own study of the passage, familiarize yourself with the leader's notes for the study you are leading.

These are designed to help you in several ways. First, they tell you the purpose the author had in mind when writing the study. Take time to think through how the study questions work together to accomplish that purpose. Second, the notes provide you with additional background information or suggestions on group dynamics for various questions. This information can be useful when people have difficulty understanding or answering a question. Third, the leader's notes can alert you to potential problems you may encounter during the study.

8. If you wish to remind yourself of anything mentioned in the leader's notes, make a note to yourself below that question in the study.

LEADING THE STUDY

1. Begin the study on time. Open with prayer.

2. Be sure that everyone in your group has a study guide.

3. At the beginning of your first time together, explain that these sessions are meant to be discussions, not lectures. Encourage the members of the group to participate. However, do not put pressure on those who may be hesitant to speak during the first few sessions. You may want to suggest the following guidelines to your group:

• Stick to the topic being discussed.

• Anything said in the group is considered confidential and will not be discussed outside the group unless specific permission is given to do so.

• Listen attentively to each other and provide time for each person present to talk.

• Pray for each other.

4. Have a group member read the introduction at the beginning of the discussion.

5. Every session begins with questions to introduce the theme of the session and encourage group members to begin to open up. Either allow a time of silence for people to respond individually or discuss it together. Be ready to get the discussion going with your own response. You may want to supplement the group discussion question with an icebreaker to help people to get comfortable.

6. Have a group member (or members, if the passage is long) read aloud the passage to be studied. Then give people several minutes to read the passage again silently so that they can take it all in.

7. As you ask the questions, keep in mind that they are designed to be used just as they are written. You may simply read them aloud. Or you may prefer to express them in your own words. There may be times when it is appropriate to deviate from the study guide. For example, a question may have already been answered. If so, move on to the next question. Or someone may raise an important question not covered in the guide. Take time to discuss it, but try to keep the group from going off on tangents.

8. Avoid answering your own questions. If necessary, repeat or rephrase them until they are clearly understood. Or point out something you read in the leader's notes to clarify the context or meaning. An eager group quickly becomes passive and silent if they think the leader will do most of the talking.

9. Don't be afraid of silence. People may need time to think about the question before formulating their answers.

10. Don't be content with just one answer. Ask, "What do the rest of

you think?" or "Anything else?" until several people have given answers to the question.

11. Acknowledge all contributions. Try to be affirming whenever possible. Never reject an answer. If it is clearly off-base, ask, "What do the rest of you think?"

12. Don't expect every answer to be addressed to you, even though this will probably happen at first. As group members become more at ease, they will begin to truly interact with each other. This is one sign of healthy discussion.

13. Don't be afraid of controversy. It can be very stimulating. If you don't resolve an issue completely, don't be frustrated. Move on and keep it in mind for later. A subsequent study may solve the problem.

14. Periodically summarize what the group has said. This helps to draw together the various ideas mentioned and gives continuity to the group. But don't preach.

15. You may want to allow group members a time of quiet for "Experiencing the Journey" or "Expressing Our Hearts to God." Then discuss what you experienced. A simple way to do this is to ask the group to pray for a few moments in silence. Then, after an appropriate amount of time, just ask, "What did you tell God?" Or you may want to encourage group members to work on these ideas between meetings. Give an opportunity during the session for people to talk about what they are learning.

16. Conclude your time together with conversational prayer, adapting the prayer suggestion at the end of the study to your group. Ask for God's help in following through on the commitments you've made.

17. End on time.

THE VERY FIRST MEETING IS IMPORTANT!

Often, it's what happens in the initial meeting that determines the culture of the group. Here's a simple outline of the first group meeting.

1. Plan on addressing some or all of the ground rules. Decide how the group will function.

2. Make sure each group member has his own guide to use.

3. Read through the introduction to the guide as a group.

4. Ask an introductory question to help foster sharing:

   • What are your expectations about being in a group like this, studying a topic like this?

   • When you look at this topic, what gets stirred up inside of you?

   • What does your wife or girlfriend, if you have one, think about your studying this?

You're ready to begin the journey toward transformation!

SESSION ONE: *The Creation of Sex*

Question 1. Give some time for the group to sit in silence to answer this question. While there may be some nervous laughter or joking, encourage the participants to sit and be courageously honest with their responses; as the leader, model an open, authentic response. Hopefully, the group will take your lead. You can be honest and ask the group to share their feelings about even being in a men's group discussing sex. Some will be nervous. Some will be eager. Some will be desperate.

Question 2. This question explores how men learn what they know about sex. Allow some story telling for men to share their exposure to sex, pornograpy, and so on.

Question 3. Try reading the passages from different translations to explore different wording and meaning. For example, *The Message* uses more specific and relevant language.

Question 6. Allow the group to compare the meaning of companionship and sex. You may want to take a piece of paper; make two columns and have the group fill in words that they think of when they think of "companionship," then "sex" and let the list you make help inform the group about how you see the differences and similarities.

Question 8. Some examples might be the intrusion of family of origin into the marital relationship, sexually transmitted disease, exploitative sexual relationships, and so on.

Question 10. Shame and guilt are important factors for men to explore in their sexual journey. Where did shame come from? How does it happen? What do we do about it as Christian men? You may want to consider additional time to explore the subject of shame and guilt within the participants. Be prepared for adding additional time or an additional session to allow the men to share, process and pray.

"Expressing Our Hearts to God." This is the first of a series of "The Naked Man's Prayers." You don't have to be literally naked or even pray this word for word! Rather, use it as a model for vulnerability in prayer. Allow time for the group to read through the prayers individually. Give time for the participants to pray and work through the prayers at their own speed. You may want to suggest that they write additional thoughts, words or sentences. Encourage them to be as specific as they can, making the prayer as personal as they feel they need to be with the prayer.

SESSION TWO: *The Fall of Sex*

Question 1. For this exercise, provide paper, pens and markers. Allow a few minutes for the participants to work alone. Then after a few minutes, ask if anyone wants to share what they have drawn. These symbols will help mark some of the events and experiences that have shaped people's identities and perhaps led them toward sexual sin. This exercise will be particularly sensitive, and many will most likely not want to share. Be prepared to offer your own example to model sharing, but allow people to pass on sharing their pictures.

Question 3. Lot snapped up the opportunity to choose first which direction and land he would settle—he picked the land that was pleasing to his eye and seemed most profitable for him. It is striking how little concern he seemed to have for Abram as he picked what seemed to him the better of two options. One has to question whether "evil desire" was really what drove Lot in his decision. Even though in 2 Peter he is called a righteous man, Lot chose to make his home in Sodom and raise his family there.

Question 7. It is striking the amount of intrigue certain sins have for each of us. Unpacking why these sins hold sway in our hearts is an important part of growing up and leaving our fallen ways for God's best.

Question 8. Very few men think they will ever have an affair, and yet a remarkable number do so. Many intend to stay sexually wholesome, but the tidal wave of hormonal and cultural pressure nudges men to make sexual decisions that affect their self-respect, their families, and their very lives. James 1:14-15 unpacks the path to destruction: "Each one is tempted when, by his own evil desire, he is dragged away and enticed. Then, after desire has conceived, it gives birth to sin; and sin, when it is full-grown, gives birth to death."

SESSION THREE: *The Redemption of Sex*

Question 1. No man can begin to know sexual transformation apart from a heart understanding of his desperate need for help that begins with a relationship with Jesus. Many men have never considered how they have failed to use their sexuality for the sake of love. Others have stories about sexual woundedness and self-centeredness that make clear the need for forgiveness and healing. No matter where you are, the clear starting place for God to redeem your sexual life is in realizing your need for His intervention. All redemption begins with the transforming power of Jesus and our faith in what he has done that we could not.

Question 2. If this question is new for you, ask yourself why. Explore the churches, men and environments that you have been exposed to that help shape your understanding of sex. Perhaps more understanding and more recollections will be triggered as you move through the sessions.

Question 8. Certain scholars have suggested that Paul is quoting someone in the Corinthian church who was making such claims. The imagery of being "mastered" suggests how certain freedoms can become distorted and the person may begin to feel like a slave.

SESSION FOUR: *Telling Your Sexual Story*

Question 1. To help you think, here are some categories to consider:

- Your mom, dad, siblings or significant others
- People who spoke into your life by their silence or by their voices or behavior about your sexuality
- Dating relationships (first loves, first sexual experience)
- Significant times where you felt warmly received or deeply rejected or betrayed
- Environments where you grew up that influenced your thinking and feeling about sex
- Experiences that you were involved with or were exposed to that had an impact
- Fantasies you had
- What you think God thinks about sex

Question 4. David uses language of blotting out, washing away and cleansing. Perhaps he is confessing that he wishes his sin had never happened, that everything could be as it was before the adultery.

Question 10. Possibilities include masturbation, homosexuality, bisexuality, Internet affairs, etc. Encourage people to think critically about what belongs on this list. Expect controversy.

SESSION SIX: *Positively Sexual*

Question 5. Author and scholar Eugene Peterson says, "We don't read very far in the Song of Songs before we realize two things: one, it contains exquisite love lyrics and two, it is very explicit sexually. The Song, in other words, makes a connection between conjugal love and sex—a very important and very biblical connection to make. . . . The Song proclaims an integrated wholeness that is at the center of

Christian teaching on committed, wedded love for a world that seems to specialize in loveless sex. . . . Despite our sordid failures in life, we see here what we are created for, what God intends for us in the ecstasy and fulfillment that is celebrated in the lyricism of the Song." Eugene Peterson, introduction to Song of Songs, in *The Message* (Colorado Springs: NavPress, 2002), p. 1182.

TRANSFORMATION
OF A MAN'S HEART *SERIES*

The Transformation of a Man's Heart series puts men in conversation with God and with one another to see how God shapes us in the ordinary experiences of our lives. The book, featuring reflections on the masculine journey by experts in a variety of fields, can be read independently or in concert with the four discussion guides, which look in depth at the role of sex, marriage, work and transformation in the spiritual lives of men.

Each guide has six sessions, suitable for personal reflection or group discussion and based on essays in the book *The Transformation of a Man's Heart*.

SEX

For all the attention we give it, sex remains a mystery. This discussion guide by Stephen W. Smith and John D. Pierce looks at sex as part of a man's transformational journey and explores how our sexual story can inform our understanding of God and his love for us.

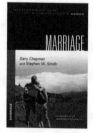

MARRIAGE

This discussion guide by Stephen W. Smith and Gary D. Chapman demystifies marriage for men, helping us see through the euphoria that led us to marry and the disillusionment that plagues us when our marriages don't turn out as we planned.

WORK

This discussion guide by Stephen W. Smith, Fil Anderson, Robert A. Fryling and Craig Glass puts men's vocational lives—their calling, their failings, their inheritance and their legacy—into the context of their relationship with God.

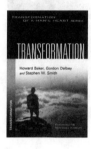

TRANSFORMATION

In this discussion guide by Stephen W. Smith, Gordon Dalbey and Howard Baker, men will be reminded that wherever they find themselves, God is there with them, inviting them out of their woundedness and onto a new and better path.

Life is many things, but it is definitely not a flow chart. We prove it every day. We deeply long for change, but formulas and seminars don't get it done. The good news is, God is at work across the life span, encouraging us and empowering us to overcome the hurdles of our past, the challenges of our present and the fears of our future.

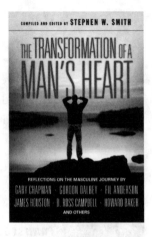

The Transformation of a Man's Heart is a book of stories: twelve men write from their hearts about their own journey toward transformation.

- Gary Chapman, author of **The Five Love Languages,** shares his journey toward experiencing a transformed marriage with his wife.

- Ross Campbell, Christian psychiatrist and author of **How to Really Love Your Child**, discusses his heart's transformation in growing as a father with his children.

- Gordon Dalbey pioneered the men's movement in his **Healing the Masculine Soul.** Here he shares how our past must be transformed in order to experience all God has for us as men.

- James Houston, mentor and friend to many Christian leaders throughout the world. considers how his own journey toward transformation reflects the call God places on every man's heart.

These and other leading men in their fields come alongside you in *The Transformation of a Man's Heart,* telling you their stories and pointing you toward the God who in the beginning wrote each of us a happy ending.

"This book is full of stories. Some will make you think.
Others will make you cry. Still others will make you kneel.
All will make you want to be a better man."

FROM THE FOREWORD BY KEN GIRE, AUTHOR OF *THE DIVINE EMBRACE*

Potter's Inn is a Christian ministry founded by Stephen W. and Gwen Harding Smith, and is dedicated to the work of spiritual formation. A resource to the local church, organizations and individuals, Potter's Inn promotes the themes of spiritual transformation to Christians on the journey of spiritual formation by offering

- guided retreats
- soul care
- books, small group guides, works of art and other resources that explore spiritual transformation

Steve and Gwen travel throughout the United States and the world offering spiritual direction, soul care and ministry to people who long for a deeper intimacy with God. Steve is the author of *Embracing Soul Care: Making Space for What Matters Most* (Kregel, 2006) and *Soul Shaping: A Practical Guide to Spiritual Transformation*.

Potter's Inn at ASPEN RIDGE is a 35-acre ranch and retreat nestled in the Colorado Rockies near Colorado Springs, CO. As a small, intimate retreat, Potter's Inn at Aspen Ridge is available for individual and small group retreats. "Soul Care Intensives"—guided retreats with spiritual direction—are available for leaders in the ministry and the marketplace.

For more information or to for a closer look at our artwork and literature, visit our website: www.pottersinn.com

Or contact us at
Potter's Inn
6660 Delmonico Drive, Suite D-180
Colorado Springs, CO 80919
Telephone: 719-264-8837
Email: resources@pottersinn.com